The Newbie's Guide to CNC Routing

Getting started with CNC machining for woodworking and other crafts.

Welcome to the world of CNC machining for woodworking and other crafts. If you've recently purchased a machine for your shop, or are just wanting to learn more before you take the plunge, this is the book for you. You'll learn the basics behind the sometimes mystifying world of these fantastic machines, how to design your projects, which tools to use, how to painlessly convert your designs into language the CNC can understand, and pick up some tips on getting started in the shop and using your CNC safely. You'll find everything in simple non-technical language, that will move you from Newbie to Novice in easy-to-understand steps.

PROF. HENRY

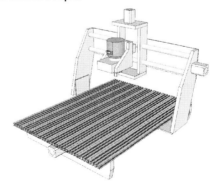

Contents

Contents *Continued*

CHAPTER 1

CNC - The Basics

What does all this "CNC" stuff mean, anyway?

CNC is a generic term meaning **Computer Numerically Controlled**, and applies to many devices including 3D printers, vinyl cutters, routers, and industrial milling machines. The movements of the device are controlled by computer instructions which tell it where to go, how to get there, and what to do.

We're woodworkers and hobby crafters so the machines we use are technically called *CNC Routers*, although we tend to use the short-hand name , **CNC**. Our CNC Routers use rotary tools to remove material from the surface of a workpiece by moving a cutter around the table in three directions.

Remember the Etch A Sketch you played with as a kid? You twisted two big knobs. One moved the stylus sideways, and one top to bottom, drawing a line on the screen. The **X-axis** of a CNC is equal to the sideways movement of the Etch A Sketch cursor, and the **Y-axis** equals the top to bottom movement. Plus, the CNC has an additional up and down movement called the **Z-axis**, giving movement in all directions.

The Etch A Sketch was fun but awkward, and most of us never succeeded in drawing anything very well. The CNC, on the other hand, by using a computer to control the cutter's movement along the three axes, can consistently and accurately cut all sorts of shapes at differing depths, in a variety of materials. Straight lines, diagonal lines, curves, circles, and holes are all easily cut with the CNC.

There are a variety of **CNC machine brands** and styles, from small to large. Yours may have been purchased or built in your shop, but whether tabletop or room size, all have some standard features.

The diagram CNC OVERVIEW labels some of the key parts and shows the movement direction along each axis. Understanding these simple parts will help our conversation as we move along.

Okay, so the computer controls the machine. How does the computer know what to do?

Well, although the CNC is a fantastic technology, it won't do anything unless it's told. It needs instructions, called *Toolpaths*, so it knows what to do. The toolpath instructions are created by software called **CAM — Computer Aided Machining** – which converts your design into code your machine understands. The most common numerical code for CNCs is called **G-code**.

You know how a GPS can tell you exactly where you are? It knows your latitude, longitude, and elevation for wherever you are on the planet. Think of the X-axis as latitude, the Y-axis as longitude, the Z-axis as elevation, and the G-code as your machine's GPS. It knows where you want to go and tells the tool how to get there, step-by-step.

Wait. I don't know anything about programming computers.

Relax. You don't have to know how to code because the CAM software you'll use to create projects does all the techie stuff for you, and generates the G-code that you'll send to your magic machine.

CNC OVERVIEW

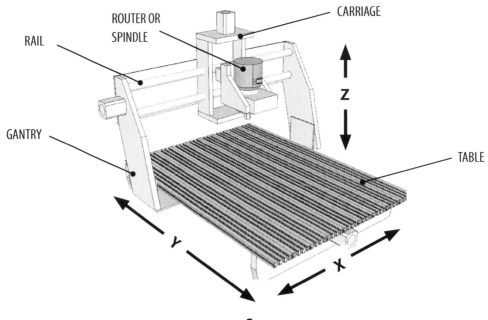

CARRIAGE

ROUTER OR SPINDLE

RAIL

Z

GANTRY

TABLE

Y

X

There is another category of software called **CAD** which stands for **Computer Aided Design.** CAD programs let us start with a drawing, a scan, a photo, or just an idea, and end up with designs to send to the CAM software. CAD creates the design **vectors** and CAM uses geometry to convert your CAD vectors to G-code.

Fortunately for us, most of the software we use is a combination of CAD and CAM, giving us the tools we need to transform sketches, photos, drawings and digital artwork into detailed **2-D**, **2.5-D** or **3-D** relief models, and then calculate toolpaths to cut these shapes accurately.

The CAM software uses a **Post Processor** setting to output the specific G-code for your machine. It's like selecting the correct driver to run a printer connected to your PC. Each printer manufacturer uses a different driver. The CNC world is the same. The Post Processor alters the G-code to match your specific machine.

There's one more step. Once you have your G-code, it goes to a **controller** that runs the machine. Some manufacturers import the code into a control device like a **pendant**. Others use controller software, like **Mach 3**, **Linux CNC**, or **Turbo CNC** to control the CNC and run the G-code from a computer.

A QUICK LOOK AT VECTORS

Vector may be a new term for you. So let's talk about that for a moment.

Remember how we said the CNC is "numerically controlled?" It needs mathematical instructions to control the movement of the cutter, and the movement needs to follow precise coordinates along a path, called a *vector*.

Vectors are the plot points the computer uses to keep track of lines, curves, and geometric shapes. Graphic designers have used vector art for years because it can be scaled up or down without losing any quality.

Most of the images you see on your computer are bitmap or raster images, which are made up of many colored pixels. JPEGs, GIFs , BMPs, and PNGs are common raster image types. Because the raster images are constructed using a fixed number of pixels or little boxes, they can't be easily re-sized, and have no path to follow.

We'll talk about converting your images to vectors later.

This sounds difficult.

Fortunately for us, most of the software we use is a combination of CAD and CAM, giving us the tools we need to transform sketches, photos, drawings and digital artwork into detailed 2-D, 2.5-D or 3-D relief models, and then calculate toolpaths to cut these shapes accurately.

Vectric Ltd has a suite of CAD/CAM software ranging from PhotoVCarve for engraving images, to V Carve with an intuitive way of designing 2-D and 2.5-D projects, and to Aspire to generate 2-D and 3-D code.

Fusion 360 by Autocad is another high-end CAD/CAM program that allows you to create sophisticated 2-D and 3-D models that you can manufacture on your CNC.

There are other CAD/CAM programs out there, but many are geared more towards high-end industrial design and machining.

Is this CAD/CAM stuff hard to learn?

There's definitely a learning curve. Using your CNC is a lot different from regular woodworking. You'll probably spend as much, or more, time on the computer as you will watching your CNC machine make the parts. But, the CAD/CAM process is the heart and soul of CNC machining, and you can't make anything without it.

The good news is that there are a lot of instructional videos and software guides to learn how to use these products. The various tools and software techniques go way beyond what we have time for here. Remember that the Internet is your friend for learning about your software options. This book is based on the assumption that your software has generated some G-code and you want to know what to do next.

THE CNC PROCESS FROM CONCEPT TO COMPLETION: CAD to CAM to CUT

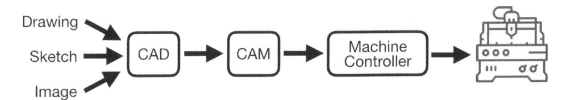

Okay, I think I know what 2-D and 3-D are, but what's this 2.5-D stuff?

A good question because most of your machining jobs will probably be 2.5-D. First, let's make sure we agree on the definition of 2-D. If you cut out a paper pattern with scissors or cut a shape on a scroll saw or bandsaw, you're making something in 2-D. The shape outline may be straight or curvy, but the surface is flat.

The Z-axis of our CNC gives us more options. CNC cutting is a subtractive process, cutting away waste material to make our part. We can tell the Z-axis how deeply to cut into the surface to make chiseled-looking carved lettering, textures, pockets, engravings, and grooves.

We call this 2.5-D since the surface isn't flat. Best of all, we can merely design in 2-D and use toolpaths to create the various depths in our project. The finished project can look like 3-D to someone who isn't familiar with the process. That's a good thing because 3-D takes a lot more time, may require more sophisticated (expensive!) software, and more design skills.

Full 3-D requires thinking, designing, and cutting in 3-D. The X, Y, and Z axes are moving simultaneously in all three directions during the 3-D cutting process, and results in sculptured-looking, contoured shapes. The cutter has to follow the defined contours in tiny steps, and machining can take hours to complete.

True 3-D creates some fantastic looking projects, and, you can often combine 2.5-D and 3-D elements in a single project to speed up production time.

The illustrations on the next page will give you a better idea of the differences between 2.5-D and 3-D machining.

A QUICK LOOK AT 2.5-D VS 3-D

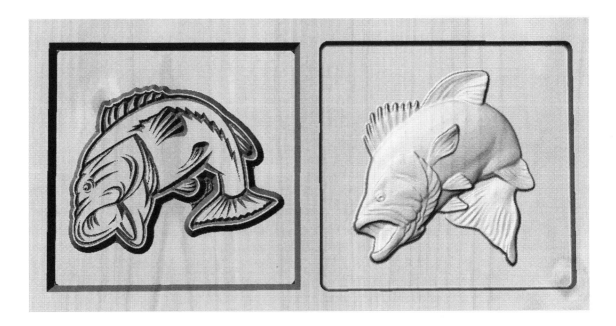

2.5-D

2.5-D machining is an effective way to give depth and dimension to otherwise flat clipart images, and is a useful method for adding artwork to signage and other projects. I looks much better than a simple silhouette.

The fish was carved with a combination of a V bit and an end mill. (*We'll talk about those in Chapter 3*)

 Machining time: about 15 minutes

3-D

The 3-D carving looks much more realistic, and sculpture-like, and works well for higher end decorative panels, finely crafted boxes, and similar projects.

The 3-D machining was done with ballnose bits using a small step-over setting. (*More about that in Chapter 3*) As noted earlier, 3-D machining is a much slower process than 2.5-D.

Machining time: 1 hour 25 minutes.

CHAPTER 2

CAD: Designing the project

How does all this work?

Okay, why don't we take a step-by-step look at making a project from start to finish?

Let's make a simple welcome sign for the front gate with the address, a name, a picture of a tree, and a cut out shape for the sign. Clip art will work for the tree, and the design software can create the sign shape and text. Using both 2-D and 2.5-D machining will make the sign more interesting.

We'll be using Vectric's V Carve CAD/CAM software to create our vectors, toolpaths, and G-code, because it's easy to understand and follow.

Uh oh, the clip art is a bitmapped image. Remember how we said a bitmapped or  raster image is made of pixels, not vectors, and we need vectors to make toolpaths? Don't worry; V Carve can convert the art to vectors for us, or we could use a program like Corel Draw, Adobe Illustrator, or even free software like Inkscape to convert bitmaps to vectors.

But what about the text? Doesn't that need to be vectors also?

Yes, it does. You're learning already. Since we're working in V Carve, it uses the fonts you have on your PC, and automatically creates outlines (vectors) of each letter.

We need to sort out some terms before we get started or it's going to get confusing. You'll be seeing the word "tool" used in two different contexts. The software has tools, and there are cutting tools designated for individual toolpaths. We'll use italics for *software tools*, and small caps for MACHINE TOOLS so we don't get lost.

One quick note before we get started: This is not a how-to guide for using Vectric's V Carve software. It's to give you an idea of how vectors and toolpaths for a CNC project are created before sending the job to the shop for production. It will help you grasp the concepts without getting bogged down in details.

We're going to size our sign so it will fit on a 1 x 12 pine board. The actual size of the wood is 3/4" thick by 11 1/4" wide, and we'll make it 16" long, so we have enough extra around the edges to secure the workpiece to the machine table to make sure it doesn't move during machining.

1 Setting up the project

The first step in V Carve is to set up the job parameters, by filling in some information.

Since we are cutting our design from only one side, our *Job Type* is Single-Sided, and the *Job Size* is the dimensions of the pine board we're using. We'll be working in inches rather than millimeters.

The *Z Zero Position* is on the top surface. Don't worry about that right now; we'll talk more about zero positions later.

The *X, Y Datum Position* is the zero point for the X and Y axes. Putting the zero point in the center makes it easier to align all the vectors to the center of the material block during the design process. We can always change it later when preparing the files for machining.

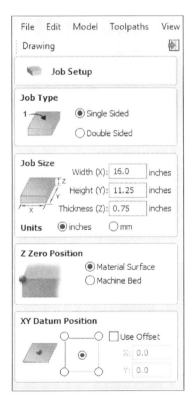

Job Setup dialog

Why would I need to change the X, Y zero point later?

You may never need to change the zero point position if you have a small hobby-sized machine. On a larger machine holding bigger sheets of material, it may be awkward to reach to the center for zeroing the machine and changing tools between toolpaths. Setting the zero point to one of the corners can make access more convenient when the router/spindle moves back to the zero point at the end of each toolpath.

2 Creating the sign shape

Now that the job setup is defined, we can see the size of our sign block on the screen, with guidelines showing where the X and Y axes meet in the middle.

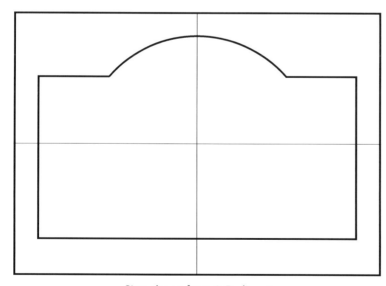

Sign shape from 2-D clipart

V Carve Clipart menu

Selecting one of the standard 2-D clip art shape vectors in V Carve works for the sign's shape, we'll use the *Scaling Tool* to make it 14" wide, and then align it to the center of the job blank.

3 Let's add a border

There is an *Offset Vectors* layout tool that creates a new vector shape offset inwards, outwards or both from a selected vector.

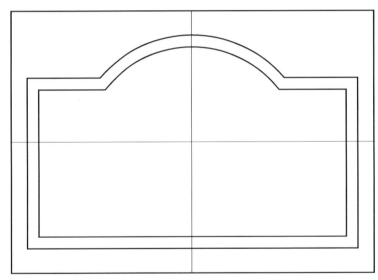

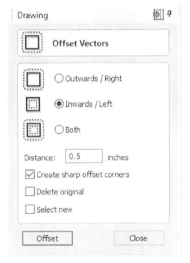

Inside border added

When we offset our sign outline inwards a half an inch, we end up with an accurate inset border vector without having to draw anything. You'll see how we use that border when we make our *toolpaths* in Chapter 4.

You'll find the *Offset Vectors* tool helpful as you gain experience in a CAD program. It's a quick and easy way, for example, to add a border around text or other artwork.

4 Importing the clip art

Our clipart tree is a bitmapped image, so we'll use V Cave's *Import Bitmap* button to load it into our file.

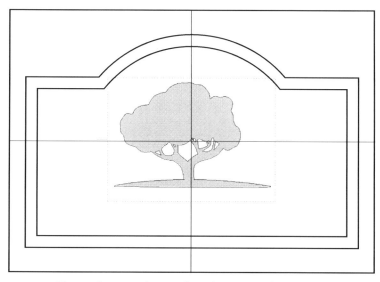

Bitmap imported, traced, and converted to vectors

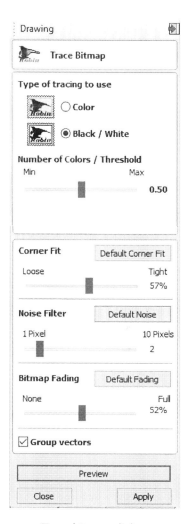

Trace bitmap dialog

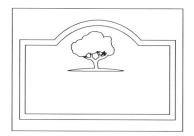

Tree vectors resized and moved

After importing, V Carve's *Trace Bitmap Tool* traces or fits vectors to both black and white or color images so they can be machined. The dialog box options help you get the best trace for your image.

The bitmapped image can be deleted after tracing, and the new vectors scaled to size and moved it into position to make room for the text.

5 Adding the text

The *Create Text Tool* brings up a dialog box where we can choose the font, the alignment, and the size. Size isn't critical because the text can be easily scaled up or down, made narrower or wider, or shorter or taller after we have placed it on the job block.

For this project, we're using the same font in two sizes. Fonts are part of the PC's font library, and we can add

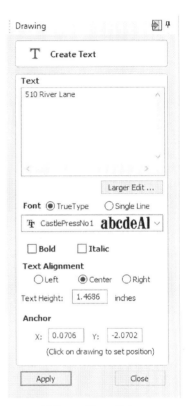

V Carve Text dialog

Text added in two sizes

more whenever we want a greater selection for design styles. We're making the address large, and the name smaller.

Layers keep things organized

V Carve has a layer function for effectively managing 2-D vectors. Yes, our design is only 2-D at the moment. We will turn it into 2.5-D when we create our toolpaths.

Isolating vectors onto a layer makes it easier to select them for assigning toolpaths. Sometimes it's helpful to duplicate a vector onto another layer so you can experiment with changes without messing up the original.

On a complex project, you can assign vectors, like text or shapes, to a separate layer, allowing you to turn them on and off as needed, making it easier to see and work with other vectors.

With a vector selected, you have the option of either Copying or Moving it to another layer, and the pull-out sub-menu allows you to pick an existing layer or create a new one.

The V Carve Layers menu shown above gives helpful visual clues about the status of each layer. When the name is **bold**, it means the layer is the active layer where you are working.

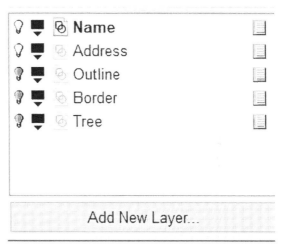

V Carve Layers menu

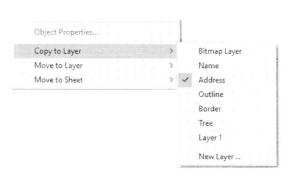

V Carve Copy or Move menu

The bright light bulb indicates the layer is visible, and the dark light bulb means the layer is hidden. You click your mouse on the light bulb icon to turn a layer on or off and click on a layer name to make it the active layer.

This project has five layers: Name, Address, Outline, Border, and Tree. The layers will make it simple to select vectors when we define the toolpaths in Chapter 4

Well, that seems pretty easy.

It is pretty easy, isn't it? Yes, we skipped a lot of details about working in V Carve, but you can see that we designed all the vectors needed for our sign in about five steps.

First, we set up the job size and defined the zero coordinates. Then we used some handy 2-D vector art in the software's library for a sign shape, and used that vector to create an inset border. Next we imported a simple clipart bitmapped image and changed it to vectors, and finally, we added some text using the same font in different sizes.

A more complex design with many vectors that have to be connected, trimmed, clipped, combined, reflected, rotated, or distorted will take more time and require a higher skill level, but the basic design principles are the same.

Creating the vector road map for toolpaths to follow is nothing mysterious, and nothing to fear.

Don't worry if our design looks a little plain right now. We're going to fix that shortly.

CHAPTER 3
A Look at CNC Tools

How do I know which tool to use with which cut?

You've hit on probably the most perplexing question in the mind of every beginner in the CNC world. What tools can I use, and what do they do? Finding the answer can be confusing because much of the CNC language came from earlier machine tools, so for woodworkers, many of the words are new.

Yeah, I keep hearing about end mills, but I don't know what they are.

In the pre-CNC days, machinists used milling machines to cut and shape parts out of solid blanks, and they called the rotary tools used in the machines, mills. End mills are rotary tools that cut with both the bottom and the sides.

I'll let you in on a secret. Those of us who aren't machinists call those rotary tools, router bits, and so do the people we buy them from.

We should talk about rotary tools for a moment. A drill bit is a rotary tool that only cuts with the up and down motion of the drill. Mills and router bits are designed to move sideways through the material and cut using the flutes on the edges. A sure way to break a drill bit is to try to cut with the side rather than the tip because the drill bit's flutes are only for removing the debris during drilling.

Most CNC router bits are able to plunge into the surface like a drill bit, before moving laterally, but experienced users, especially when cutting with small diameter bits, often ramp them into the material. Ramping means entering the material at an angle, so the cut depth is approached gradually rather than plunging straight in. You can tell the CNC to ramp a cut when you set up the toolpath for a tool.

Let's take a quick look at the anatomy of router bits so we can learn some terms that will help our discussion later when we add tools to our CAM software database.

Anatomy of a spiral end mill

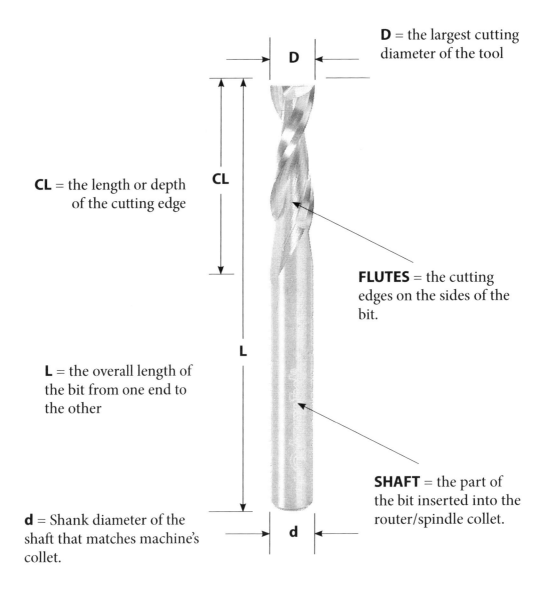

D = the largest cutting diameter of the tool

CL = the length or depth of the cutting edge

FLUTES = the cutting edges on the sides of the bit.

L = the overall length of the bit from one end to the other

SHAFT = the part of the bit inserted into the router/spindle collet.

d = Shank diameter of the shaft that matches machine's collet.

Photo © Amana Tool®

Anatomy of a V groove router bit

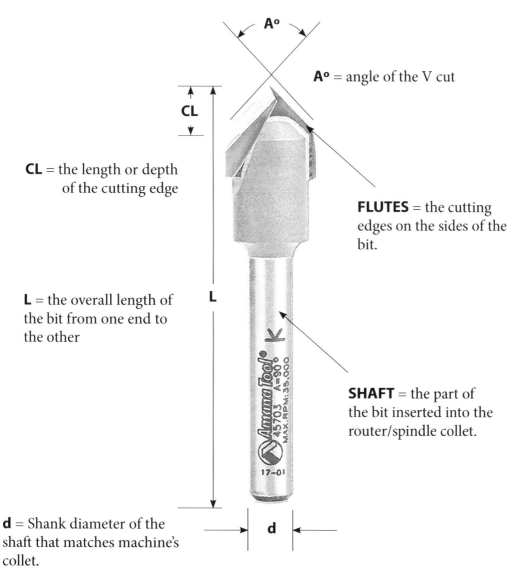

A° = angle of the V cut

CL = the length or depth of the cutting edge

FLUTES = the cutting edges on the sides of the bit.

L = the overall length of the bit from one end to the other

SHAFT = the part of the bit inserted into the router/spindle collet.

d = Shank diameter of the shaft that matches machine's collet.

So I can use regular router bits in a CNC?

Yes. The materials most of us will be cutting include wood, plastics, dense foam board, and maybe some soft non-ferrous metals like brass or aluminum. Choosing the correct bit can improve CNC machining, and there are bits specifically designed for cutting plastic and aluminum.

There are different geometries to be considered also. You can see the obvious difference between the spiral bit and the V bit shown earlier, but you may be unaware that there are different spiral bits.

Up-cut spiral bit
Photo © Amana Tool®

Spiral bits

Spiral bits are flat-bottomed cutters, leaving a smooth flat surface. An up-cutting spiral is the most common, and the flutes pull the waste to the top of the material being cut. This bit can lift the stock away from the table, so secure clamping is essential.

The up-cut spiral also tends to pull wood fibers up around the edge of the cut causing tearing or splintering on the top surface. Single flute upcut bits are the best choice for cutting plastics so the waste material is pulled out quickly before it can re-weld into the cut.

Tear-out from an up-cut spiral bit

Down-cut spiral

A remedy for rough edges is the down-cut spiral that pushes the waste down into the cut, leaving smooth, fuzz-free edges on the surface, and driving the material down onto the CNC table (you'll still need clamping). Down-cut spirals can be helpful when cutting out parts because any tear-out or roughness is on the back or bottom surface.

Down-cut spiral bit
Photo © Amana Tool®

Compression bit

This brings us a third style, the compression bit. Compression bits have both up-cut and down-cut spiral flutes specially designed to eliminate tearing or chipping on both surfaces. It is excellent for creating grooves or dado cuts in plywood, MDF, and other composites.

The most commonly used end-mill sizes for woodworking on the CNC are 1/4" and 1/8", although larger and smaller sizes less than 1/16th of an inch can be used if you have a collet that can hold the appropriate shaft. End mills are useful for pockets or mortises, cutting parts out of the stock, and roughing out a 3-D or V carving before the finishing pass.

Compression bit
Photo © Amana Tool®

V-bits

V groove or V carving bits are generally just called V-bits. They are the go-to tool for sign carving and engraving or chamfering an edge. The bits are designated by the angle of the cut, and a wide range of angles are available ranging from 15° to 140°. Most bits end at a point, but some are available with a squared off bottom where the flutes meet. The angles most commonly used are the 60° and 90°. We'll talk about why you need multiple V-bit in the next chapter.

V groove bits
Photo © Amana Tool®

Ballnose bits

Ballnose bits have a rounded cutting tip, and they are the style bits used for 3-D carving. The rounded tip minimizes tool marks to produce smooth contours on 3-D projects. They can also be useful for sign making when you want a rounded bottom in the carved letters.

Like the endmills, ballnose bits are available in a range of cutting diameters. Often, in the smaller sizes, like 1/16", the bit body is tapered to give it more strength.

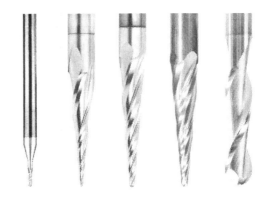

Tapered and standard ballnose bits
Photo © Amana Tool®

20

Surfacing bits

At some point, you'll want to invest in a surfacing bit. These bits cut a wide area and are used to flatten the spoilboard on our machines (more about this in Chapter 5) or planing large glued up panels.

Surfacing bit
Photo © Amana Tool®

Other choices

Round-over bits, plunge-style ogee, and other contour bits can be used on the CNC, but you should experiment with the simple bits first. You'll be surprised at the contour shapes you can create with ballnose, V, and spiral bits used alone or in a combination.

#56126

Photo © Amana Tool®

Some bits aren't for your CNC

You won't be using pattern, flush trim, or chamfer bits on your CNC, or any other bit with a bearing. The bearings on these bits are intended to ride along the edge of the stock to ensure an even cut. The CNC easily controls the cutting action of the bits and needs no help to guide it along the work.

Photo © Amana Tool®

Choosing a bit size

Bits are available in different shank sizes. The most common Imperial sizes are 1/8", 1/4", and 1/2". The larger shank sizes are ideal because they are stronger and more able to withstand the strong lateral forces with the CNC.

Your choice of shank diameter will be constrained by the collet or collets available for your machine. You'll need bits with a long enough cutting length to cut through your material, but it's best to use the shortest possible overall length to prevent vibration and deflection.

So, I just pick the bit I want, and I'm good to go?

No, not quite. There are other variables we need to consider if we are going to get optimal performance out of our CNC. We have to balance the desire for speed with the demand for smooth cuts, plus decide how deeply we can cut in one pass, based on the hardness of our material, and what speed our bit should be spinning.

Bit material

Router bits are available in three styles: High-Speed Steel (HSS), Carbide-tipped, and Solid Carbide. High-speed steel dulls quickly and is not a good choice. Both Carbide-tipped and Solid carbide work well, and either is a good choice.

You also want to choose a bit that will give you the best results with the shortest machining time.

The mystery of feeds, speeds, and chip loads.

Feed is how fast the cutter is pushed through the material by the machine and is usually measured in inches per minute (ipm).

Speed is the rpm of the router or spindle, which tells us how fast the cutter is spinning. Spindle speeds can be controlled by software and router speeds can be manually set if they have a variable speed function.

Chip load is the thickness, or bite, of material removed by one cutting edge of the cutter as it rotates along the toolpath.

These three factors work together to produce the CNC's cutting action. Speeds that are too slow can generate heat that will dull the bits faster and may cause burn marks on the stock. Speeds moving too quickly can stress the cutter and cause it to break. Breakage is not a good idea with a bit spinning at 10,000 to 20,000 rpm.

What we're after is the sweet spot of feed and speed that gives us smooth cuts in a reasonable time. Fortunately, for us woodworkers, the sweet spot is rather large and less demanding.

Some simple math and some chip load charts will give us the answers we need for efficient machining by adjusting the feeds and speeds. Let's take a look at the formulas

$$\textbf{Chip Load} = \frac{\text{Feed Rate}}{\text{RPM x Number of Flutes}}$$

$$\textbf{Feed Rate} = \text{RPM x Number of Flutes x Chip Load}$$

$$\textbf{RPM} = \frac{\text{Feed Rate}}{\text{Number of Flutes x Chip Load}}$$

The three ways to increase the chip load are: increase the feed rate, decrease the spindle speed (rpm), and/or use a bit with fewer flutes.

The CNCs most of us are using for woodworking and crafting have limited feed rate capabilities compared to the large industrial production machines. The top rpm for the spindles available for our machines is around 10,000, and for routers,

Freud® Chip Load Charts

MDF /Particle Board

Tool Diameter	Chip Load
1/8"	.004" to .007"
1/4"	.012" to .015"
1/2"	.020" to .025"

Hardwood

Tool Diameter	Chip Load
1/8"	.002" to .004"
1/4"	.005" to .007"
1/2"	.017" to .019"

Softwood/Plywood

Tool Diameter	Chip Load
1/8"	.003" to .005"
1/4"	.006" to .008"
1/2"	.019" to .021"

Soft Plastic

Tool Diameter	Chip Load
1/8"	.003" to .005"
1/4"	.006" to .009"
1/2"	.011" to .014"

Hard Plastic

Tool Diameter	Chip Load
1/8"	.002" to .004"
1/4"	.005" to .008"
1/2"	.010" to .013"

in the neighborhood of 25,000 rpm. And, the feed rate of our machines is generally under 200 ipm while those of industrial machines can range as high as 1,000 ipm or more.

A word about flutes: **More flutes does NOT equal a better finish.** More flutes make more chips, and the CNC has to travel faster to eject them.

We can't achieve the feed rates of high-end CNCs, so we're better off sticking with bits having one or two flutes.

Where do I get this chip load information?

Some of the manufacturers provide chip load information about each individual bit, but the data in the tables on the previous page will get you started.

Remember, these are just the recommended targets. You will want to adjust your answers to suit your machine, your bits, and the material you are cutting.

You can fine-tune your cuts by starting with the recommended chip load and slowly increasing the feed rate until the cut finish is unacceptable. Slow the feed rate again until your finish is okay once again, then gradually reduce the rpm until the finish deteriorates. At that point, increase the speed until the finish is restored.

Write down the speed and feed information in your notebook because you've reached the sweet spot for the bit you're using, and the material you're cutting.

Do I really need to know all this stuff?

Yes. You will produce better work as you gain experience with your machine, your cutting tools, and the material you're cutting if you learn how to apply these simple principles.

The short answer

Sticking with bits that have no more than two flutes, and using a middle-of-the-road spindle speed and feed rate will get you through most of your woodworking projects.

Where things are stable in the metal cutting world, we woodworkers have a lot more variables affecting our cuts, including wood moisture, grain, and differences in hardness. Most of us aren't in the mass production world either, so production speed is less of an issue.

In short, chip loads, speeds, and feed rates give us a good starting point but don't need to be strictly adhered to. You'll get better at it as you gain experience.

45° V bit @ 16,500 rpm - 33 ipm

45° V bit @ 16,500 rpm - 66 ipm

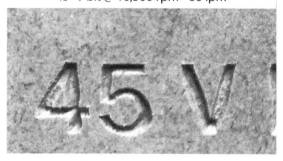

45° V bit @ 16,500 rpm - 100 ipm

Actual carving size

Testing is Easy

Here an enlarged look at a simple speed and feed test cut into MDF. The letters in the text are 0.3" tall and carved with a 45°, single-flute V bit, at 16,500 rpm.

The letters have crisp edges and corners when cutting at 33 ipm, and you can see how the corners of the letters degrade as the feed speed increases to 100 ipm.

A test like this only takes a few minutes and should be done on the same material you'll be using in your project. The few minutes you spend getting the correct feeds and speeds can save you disappointment later.

Keep an accurate record by using the Speed and Feed Test Record pages in the back of the book.

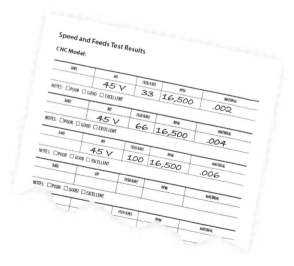

The Tool Database

One of the ways you'll be using the speed and feed information is with your CAM software's Tool Database.

The Tool Database is your library of available tools for performing cutting operations on your CNC, and you'll use it when creating the toolpaths for your project. Accurate information about each tool ensures that you'll get the cutting results you are expecting.

The tool description examples below are from Vectric's V Carve software, and you can see that different information is needed for different styles of bits. Initially, you might use the default information included in the software for various bit styles, but you'll want to update that information as you gain experience with your own machine, bits, and materials.

Naming the tool is important because you'll want to make sure you are selecting

Vectric's V Carve Pro Tool Database

the correct tool both during the CAM process and later in the shop. For example, it's a good idea to indicate in the name if an endmill is an up-cut or down-cut. If you have V bits with the same angle but varying cutting widths, it's a good idea to add the width of cut to the name.

Note the differences in diameter settings. For the endmill, the diameter means the diameter of the shaft. For the V bit, the diameter is the width of the cutting head. The angle setting for the V bit is the angle of the cut, but when entering a V-shaped engraving bit with a flat tip, you'll only enter one side, or one half, of the cutting angle. Don't worry if this sounds confusing. Your software will guide you.

Pass depth is how deep the bit can plunge into the material in one pass. A large CNC can easily cut to a depth equal to the diameter of the bit, but on smaller machines, you are better off starting with a depth equal to half the diameter. You can speed production by increasing the cut depth once you determine your CNC can handle the increased stress

Stepover is how far the bit moves sideways from the first cut when it comes along to take more material. When cutting pockets, for example, each subsequent cut needs to overlap the first so that all the material is removed. The V bit needs more stepover

information because it may be used in 3D carving which requires tighter tolerances for finishing cuts. A finishing stepover setting is usually less than 10% of the bit diameter.

We've already talked about **spindle speeds and feed rates,** so you know what information goes there.

Plunge rate is how quickly the bit drops into the material, and moving too fast may damage the bit or the material. Plunge rate is another area to test. You may find making the plunge rate closer to the feed rate will significantly shorten machining time.

Tool Number won't be important for most of us, because it is for CNC's with automatic tool changers. If your machine has a changer you can add a tool number here. For the rest of us, any number will do.

Now that we have a good idea about the various types of cutters, how to calculate their speeds and feeds, and how to enter the information in our tool library database, it's time to put all this information to work.

CHAPTER 4

CAM: Putting it all together

Combining tools and vectors to build toolpaths

You probably got glassy-eyed in that last chapter as you waded through learning about different tools (router bits), and how to calculate their speeds, feeds, and chip loads. It's time to have some fun, and actually, put all that information to work.

We completed our design in Chapter 2, and now we're going to start creating the paths that the tools will follow on the CNC. These toolpaths are what will move us from our computer design to a tangible product. We'll use some different types of cuts, and some different TOOLS to add dimension to our dull, flat-looking vector image.

We'll be using Vectric's V Carve's software, once again, to create our toolpaths. You'll find similar tool operations in other CAM programs.

But first, let's define some terms before we get started.

Profile Toolpath

With a Profile cut, the cutter follows a vector and cuts either along or on the line. The cut can be made on the vector, outside, or inside when cutting a closed shape like a circle. The tool will cut on, to the left, or to the right when cutting open vectors. The software compensates for the diameter and tool angles when defining the toolpath.

Pocketing Toolpath

Pockets are just what they sound like, a recessed area below the surface of the material. In conventional woodworking, a mortise would be an example of a pocket, as would the inside of a small box.

Drilling Toolpath

The drilling toolpath allows a hole to be drilled at a set depth based on the center of the closed vector. You can set the toolpath to do a peck drilling operation which drills down slightly, pulls out to remove the waste and then returns to cut a little deeper, repeating the action until the set depth is reached.

V Carve Toolpath

This toolpath uses the V-bits we discussed earlier to either cut to the full depth between two vectors as you might have when cutting the letters in text, or you can cut to a set depth. We'll talk in more detail about V Carve toolpaths shortly.

Texture Toolpath

You can create some interesting textures for your project with this toolpath which calculates vectors for the tool to follow. You can create a wide variety of textures by experimenting with various tools and tool sizes.

Roughing Toolpath

This is used when machining 3-D parts and clears away a lot of excess material quickly so the finishing tool which is usually smaller, can carve the 3D elements in a single pass.

Finishing Toolpath

This is the follow-up to the roughing path and carves smoothly sculptured 3-D parts.

Other Toolpath options

There are other toolpaths available such as engraving, inlay, fluting, prism carving, and molding. Refer to your CAD software to learn more about these toolpaths. For now, we're going to see what can accomplish with just a few of the toolpath choices.

I'm getting curious about how these toolpaths actually look.

Okay, let's start with a simple v-carved version of our sign. This style of sign can be done with freehand routing, but it's easier and more accurate on the CNC.

Remember what our vector drawing looks like? There are outlines of the tree, some text, a border, and the sign shape.

We could use a *V Carve* and *Profile* toolpath for everything, and end up with a sign that looks like the letters and art were chip-carved into the wood, and as you can see, the result is okay but boring.

A simple V-carved sign

Our sign still looks pretty much 2-D. We need to spice it up.

Moving from 2-D to 2.5-D

We can add dimension to our sign by cutting the background away from the address, tree, and border to make them raised.

If you remember, we used layers when we created our sign, and using them now will make it easy to select the vectors needed for this first toolpath.

We'll use the vectors on the address, tree, and border layers to set up a V-Carve

toolpath to give a nice angled cut to all the edges of the art and text.

The dark lightbulbs show us the Name and Outline layers are turned off at the moment.

We're going to use a *V-Carve /Engraving Toolpath* to carve away the background around our selected vectors.

Vectors selected for Address, Tree, and Border

1 Carving the background

Our material is 3/4" thick so let's carve the background down 1/4" using a 60° V-bit.

The start depth is set at 0.0 inches which is the surface of our material. The Flat Depth box is checked and set to 0.25 inches, and we selected the 60° V-bit from out tool database.

Trying to clear out so much material for the background would be time-consuming and challenging with the pointed end of the V-bit, so we need to add a *Flat Area Clearance* tool that allows us to clear

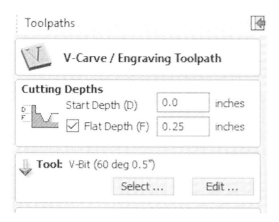

a large area to a flat depth with a flat-bottomed cutter like an endmill. Let's use the 1/4" Up-cut spiral bit from our *Tool Database*.

We need to make one more setting for the *Flat Area Clearance*, telling the machine what kind of path to follow when clearing background.

 An *Offset* path starts in the center and works its way to the edges. A *Raster* path moves back and forth. We'll use a Raster cut with the angle setting at 0.0°, so the cut runs along the wood in the same direction as the grain which helps hide the tool marks and makes finishing easier.

When we save our toolpath, we actually end up with two toolpaths. One for the *Flat Area Clearance*, and one for the *V-carve*. We can use V Carve's Preview to check how they will perform on the CNC.

V-carve (Pocket) toolpath

 We specified a 1/4" endmill for the *Flat Area Clearance*. The gray area shows where the toolpath cleared most of the waste away, getting as close as it could to the detailed areas around the type and tree.

Note how the toolpath cut everything inside the border, and to the outside of the tree and text. Had we failed to select the border when defining the toolpath, the trees and letters would have been cleared on the inside of their vectors.

Flat Area Clearance toolpath Preview

V-carve toolpath

 Previewing the 60° *V-carve toolpath* we can see how it adds a bevel to the inside of the border, the outline of the tree, and bevels and cuts all the details in the text.

V-Carve Address toolpath Preview

2 Carving the name

Now that we've cut the pocket for the raised letters and tree using an end mill and V-bit let's select the text for the name and carve it into the background.

We'll set up another *V-Carve/ Engraving toolpath*, using the same 60° v-bit, and since we've carved the background down 1/4", we need to set that as our Start Depth; otherwise we would only be cutting air.

32

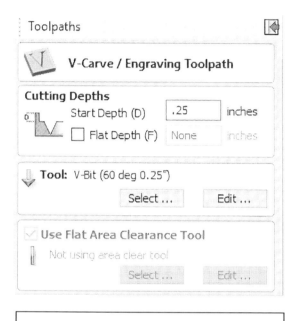

Vectors selected for Name

Wait! You didn't set a Flat Depth of cut for the text.

Good catch! But, we don't have to set the depth for a standard *V-carve* because the bit can only cut as deeply as the outlines allow.

When you put a funnel into the neck of a bottle, it can just go so far before the angle of the funnel's sides makes it wider than the opening, and it can't go any deeper into the bottle.

The vector outlines of the letters are like the bottle opening, and the V-bit is like the angled sides of the funnel. The bit can only carve down until it hits the outlines that are the edges of the letters.

But, what if I want the letters carved deeper?

That's why we need to have a variety of V-bits in our collection. A 45° V-bit will carve deeper than a 60°, which will cut deeper than a 90°, and a 120° bit makes an even shallower cut.

Angle of bit changes depth of cut

33

The combination of our font size and the 60° bit we're using gives us letters carved about 3/16" deep. And, remember, we're starting our carving at the quarter-inch depth of the main pocket, so we're actually cutting about 7/16" into our piece of wood. Since our sign blank is 3/4" thick, we don't have any problems, but if it were thinner, say 1/2", we would want to use the 90° bit, to eliminate any chance of cutting all the way through the sign.

The **Name** toolpath appears on the list after we tell V Carve to calculate it, and

the preview shows our sign is looking pretty good.

V-Carve Name toolpath Preview

Our sign is almost finished. There's just one more step. We need to view the Outline layer and select the vector for the sign's shape.

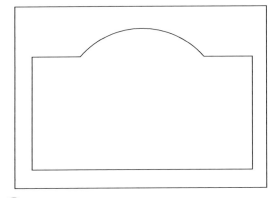

3 Cutting out the shape

It's back to the 1/4" end mill for this operation. We'll use a *Profile* toolpath to cut out the sign's shape, and select the upcut endmill from the Tool Database.

Once again the Start Depth is zero because we're starting on the surface.

Pay close attention to the depth of cut. It is set to the thickness of our sign blank, and it will cut all the way through. You can set the depth to a few thousandths of an inch deeper than the thickness to ensure you cut all the way through, but be cautious you don't inadvertently cut into your CNC's table.

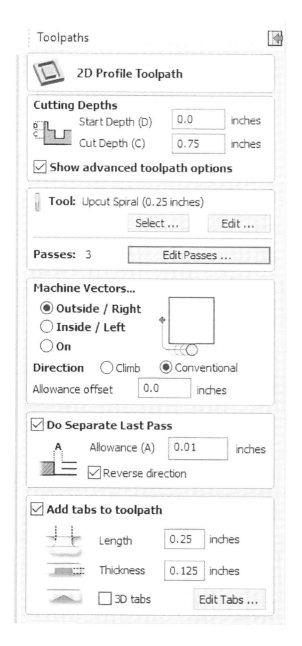

Toolpaths

2D Profile Toolpath

Cutting Depths

Start Depth (D) 0.0 inches

Cut Depth (C) 0.75 inches

☑ Show advanced toolpath options

Tool: Upcut Spiral (0.25 inches)

Select ...   Edit ...

Passes: 3   Edit Passes ...

Machine Vectors...

◉ Outside / Right
○ Inside / Left
○ On

Direction ○ Climb ◉ Conventional

Allowance offset 0.0 inches

☑ **Do Separate Last Pass**

A Allowance (A) 0.01 inches

☑ Reverse direction

☑ **Add tabs to toolpath**

Length 0.25 inches

Thickness 0.125 inches

☐ 3D tabs   Edit Tabs ...

The tool is cutting in 3 passes because the pass depth in the database is set to .25".

We are cutting on the outside of the vector. If we cut **on** the vector the sign would be 1/8" (half the diameter of the bit) smaller, and 1/4" smaller if we cut **inside** the vector. Both of those options would make the border narrower than our design.

By adding a *Separate Last Pass*, the tool will cut slightly larger for most of the passes and then move into the line for the last pass, giving a cleaner cut and eliminating excess tool marks.

The *Tabs* box allows us to set up small tabs that won't cut all the way through the material. They are essential because without them the cutout sign has nothing holding it in place and if it moves the cutter will gouge the edge at the very least, and could damage the cutter.

Tabs prevent sign from breaking free

35

Here's how our final sign looks after cutting off the tabs.

Finished sign preview

That's a lot better than the plain v-carved version.

It sure is, and we did it with only two tools, a 1/4" endmill and the same 60° v-bit we used in the earlier version. The entire sign is carved with only four toolpaths.

But, let's give this sign more flair. We can do that by adding one more toolpath.

4 Adding a background texture

Vectric's V Carve software has a *Texture Toolpath* that will let us easily add a background texture to our sign.

Textures can be calculated inside any selected vector boundaries or, if nothing is selected, across the entire job size.

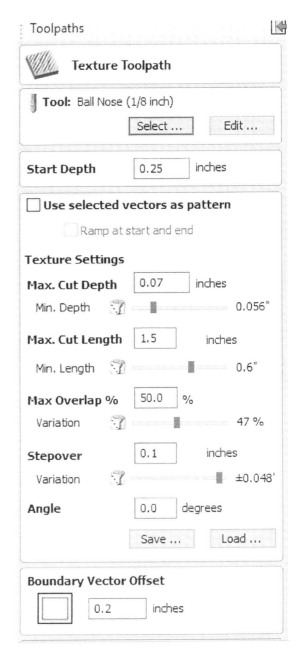

We're using a 1/8" Ball Nose bit from our Tool Database. The start depth is .25" because we're starting at the depth we carved for our background.

The texturing options calculate random patterns and the settings may appear a little complicated.

The best way to see what effect each variable has on the texture is to change the numbers, calculate and preview the results until you have a texture you like.

You could draw vectors for the texture to follow, but we're going to use the random pattern created by the settings.

We will use a *Boundary Vector Offset*, so the texture doesn't damage our text or border. The value in this field offsets

the texturing from the boundary by the specified amount. Usually, the diameter of your bit is sufficient, but our v-carved text requires us to leave a little extra room. The boundary vectors are our border, the address, the tree, and the name.

And, here's the *Ta-Da!* moment. With one additional toolpath, we moved our sign into the *Wow!* category.

We've come a long way from that simple v-carved version, haven't we?

Texture boundaries

We've created all of our toolpaths and previewed them, so we know how they will cut on our CNC. Now there's one more vital step: saving our toolpath G-code.

We'll use V Cave's *Save Toolpaths* button to change our digital paths into something our machine can recognize.

We can't use the *Output all visible toolpaths to one file* option because they are different tools; an endmill, a v-bit, and a ballnose bit.

Make sure you have selected the correct Post Processor for your CNC before you click the save button.

That's it. Once you've saved your toolpaths, you're ready to head to the shop and start making sawdust.

We've talked about the basics of CNC machining, learned how to create a project with CAD software, discussed the different types of tools, how to calculate their feeds and speeds, and finally, created toolpaths with CAM software.

It's time to move from the digital to the physical world, and talk about what we need to know in the shop.

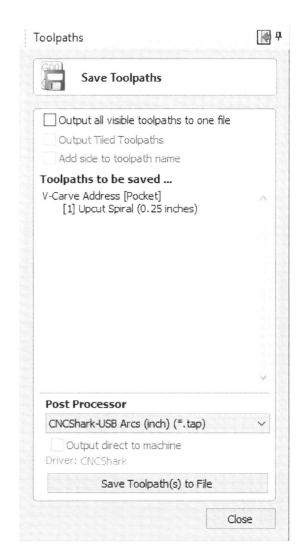

38

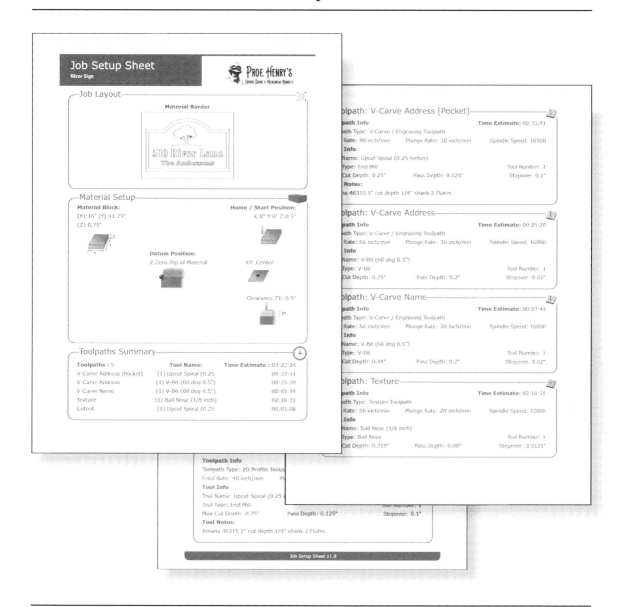

Vectric's V Carve Pro and Aspire programs can create a Job Summary sheet that is very helpful in the shop. It's easy to forget which bit you planned for a toolpath, so a written reminder comes in very handy. Just ask those of us who inadvertently used a 90º v-bit instead of the 60º our toolpath was planned for, or a 1/8" endmill instead of a 1/4".

CHAPTER 5

Getting ready

Things to do before starting your first CNC project

I know, I know. You're chomping at the bit and ready to slap some material on the machine and get down to business. You've had enough of this techie-talk, and dying to see some chips flying.

Slow down. We're not quite ready yet.

First, it's time for the obligatory safety message. You know, like the one you always tune out on the airplane but wish you'd listened to when the plane suddenly hits severe weather, and you're knuckles are turning white on the armrest?

Your CNC machine, like other woodworking tools, can be dangerous. There are incredibly sharp pieces of metal, whirling around and around at thousands of revolutions per minute while moving in three dimensions against material you're hoping doesn't move, but can before you realize what's happening.

A moment of inattention can cause the cutter to crash into your CNC's table, a

hold-down clamp, or allow your workpiece to move unexpectedly, resulting in a broken tool, a destroyed table, a ruined project, or a trip to the emergency room.

There's no reason to fear your new shop helper, just give it the love and respect it deserves. And, as with all other power tools, use appropriate safety equipment like eye, ear, and dust protection.

Okay, safety message over. Let's get back to work.

INSTALLING A SPOILBOARD

What's a spoilboard?

Well, they should probably be called non-spoilboards or un-spoilboards, because they protect your CNC's table from being damaged by the cutting tool when you're cutting all the way through the material to make a shape like the outline on our sign project.

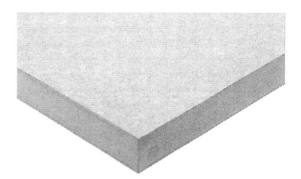

Medium Density Fiberboard (MDF)

In short, spoilboards are a sacrificial top for your CNC table that can be resurfaced or replaced as needed. It should be large enough to cover your CNC's cutting area.

Generally, spoilboards are made out of 3/4" thick MDF (Medium Density Fiberboard) because it is stable, flat, dense, durable, and inexpensive. MDF doesn't have the seasonal contraction and expansion problems encountered with natural woods.

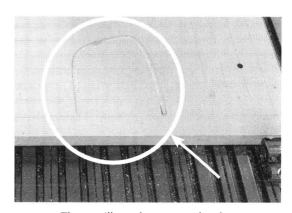

The spoilboard can save the day when things go wrong

Another option used by some is LDF (Low-Density Fiberboard) which is lighter in weight than MDF, and a few others use HDPE (High-Density Polyethylene) which has a high strength to density ratio but is much more expensive and somewhat less versatile.

MDF is also porous enough to allow air to pass through, making it an excellent choice for vacuum hold-down systems.

How do I attach the spoilboard to my CNC's table?

The easiest and most secure method is with through bolts that securely attach the spoilboard to your CNC's table. Nylon bolts are highly recommended because you'll never damage a bit if you accidentally hit a bolt head during a tooling operation.

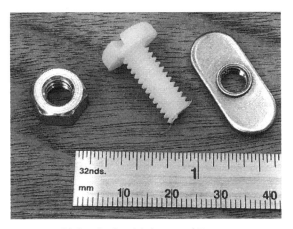

Nylon bolt with hex and T-nuts

Recessing the bolt heads below the spoilboard's top surface ensures the cutter won't run into one and allows you to resurface the spoilboard multiple times before it needs replacing. Pan head bolts can be used without a washer and will hold well. If your CNC has a T-track table, T-nuts work well with the bolts to keep the spoilboard in place.

The number of hold-down bolts needed will vary depending on the size of your cutting area. You'll want some spaced around the edges at the very least, and probably in the central area of your spoilboard to make sure it lays flat.

Recess the bolt head below the surface as shown in this cutaway view

Aligning the spoilboard

Your CNC's table is generally larger than the cutting area, so we need to make sure the spoilboard is in the correct spot before we fasten it down.

a V-bit helps align the spoilboard

The easiest way to do this is to install a V-bit or a small diameter endmill, and manually jog your cutter head to the lower left corner of its cutting area without the spindle or router running.

Position the lower left corner of the spoilboard at that spot. Then you can traverse the X, and then the Y axis to check that the edges of the spoilboard are square to the machine's travel.

When you're satisfied that everything is square, tighten down the bolts.

So, with my spoilboard installed, I'm good to go?

Not yet. We need to eliminate two factors that can spoil an otherwise well-planned project.

First, although MDF is stable and reasonably flat, there are always some variations in thickness across its width or length. Second, the machine's table surface may not be precisely parallel with the X, Y axes of the spindle or router's movement.

Even a difference of a few thousandths of an inch can cause a noticeable difference in the depth of cut of text and lines when using V Carve/Engraving toolpaths causing them to be too shallow in one spot and too deep in another. Pocketing and inlay operations will also suffer.

Spoilboard surfacing

With the spoilboard securely in place, we can create a simple pocketing toolpath and use a surfacing bit to skim a few thousandths of an inch off the surface. Be sure to draw the pocket outline, so the cutter cuts half of its diameter wider than the edges, so you don't leave any areas uncut. Especially at the corners.

Scribbling across the top of the spoilboard with a pencil or a marker will give you a visual reference that you have leveled the entire surface evenly. If there are still marks left after your skim cut, reset the file to cut a little deeper and run the toolpath a second time.

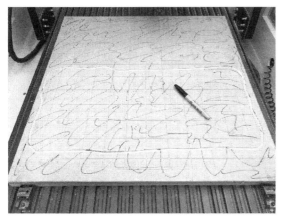

Marking the surface for a skim cut

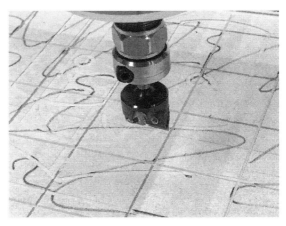

Resurfacing to renew the spoilboard

Save the file because you'll use it again at a later date when the surface of your spoilboard has become gouged and distressed by through cutting operations and screwing into it to hold material in place. You'll eventually replace your spoilboard when it gets too thin because of multiple resurfacing operations.

Some spoilboard options

With the spoilboard aligned squarely to the X and Y axes, you can quickly align your work to the spoilboard edges and know it is square for machining. But when working on smaller pieces, it's often more convenient to place them more towards the middle of the working area. That means we need a different way to square up our material for cutting.

It's easy to set up some toolpaths to cut grid lines into the surface of our spoilboard that will help align our material. A one- or two-inch grid will work well, and a 60° or 90° V-bit cutting 0.03 to 0.06 inches deep will scribe nice reference lines.

Installing threaded inserts into your spoilboard is a handy way to attach hold-down clamps when securing your work. Generally, 1/4-20 bolts work well for hold-down operations, so select an insert size that matches.

There are many styles of threaded inserts available, and they can be installed either from the top or bottom of the spoilboard. Brass inserts are recommended if the top of the insert will be anywhere close to the surface of the spoilboard. If the cutter hits an insert, brass is much more forgiving than carbide hitting a steel insert.

Alignment grid and threaded inserts

Use a screw to securely attach the work

Remember, you'll be resurfacing the spoilboard occasionally so be sure the inserts will not be too close to the surface and interfere with the cutter.

SECURING THE WORKPIECE

Preventing movement of the material is critically important with CNC machining. The bit is trying to push it in all lateral directions with the CNCs movement, and tools like an upcut endmill are trying to lift the material from the table. Things can go wrong quickly when the part being routed isn't held solidly in place.

The simplest hold-down method is a screw driven through your material and into the spoilboard. Drilling pilot holes first, may help prevent the screw from raising fibers around the screw hole in the MDF, but you can always knock those back down with a quick sandpaper hit.

Another method that works reasonably well for light material is double-sided tape. Apply a generous amount of tape to the back of your material and press it firmly to the spoilboard. Double-sided tape can be helpful when you are cutting out small parts and don't want to use tabs to keep the part connected, so it doesn't break loose at the completion of the cut.

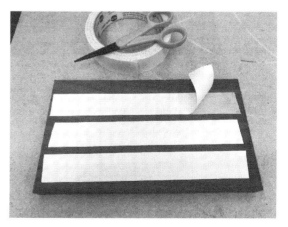

Double-sided tape can secure light pieces

Super glue & painters tape make a strong bond

T-track hold-down clamps

A tape method that has proven to be very secure is the combination of painter's tape and super glue. The tape is burnished to both the back of the material and to the spoilboard. Then a few beads of super glue are applied to the tape on either the part or the table, and the two pieces firmly pressed together for a few moments.

Regular T-track style clamps can be used if your CNC is set up for them. They apply enough pressure to secure almost any workpiece. Their drawback is that they tend to be large and clunky, sticking up quite a bit above your workpiece and the spoilboard.

The super glue welds the tape pieces together but the tape is easily removed from the part and spoilboard when machining is finished. As an added bonus, the painter's tape leaves less residue than double-sided tape.

Shop-made hold-downs

Shop-made wooden hold-downs have a lot of advantages. First of all, they are inexpensive to make out of baltic birch plywood or hardwood, and second, they are very forgiving when they have an unplanned meeting with a spinning bit. Third, they are low profile so Z clearance is less of an issue.

You could use them with screws driven into the spoilboard, but why not take advantage of those threaded inserts we talked about earlier and hold them in place with nylon bolts? By making them in various lengths, we can always reach an insert to secure the material.

Using the CNC to make hold-downs

No matter which hold-down method you use, you must be sure the hold-down is NOT in the way of any toolpath. Remember, the cutting diameter of your tool is larger than the vector line in your design. Leave plenty of clearance.

CAUTION: Z HEIGHT CLEARANCE

Setting a Z clearance height for your toolpaths tells the CNC how high to lift the bit away from the surface while it moves from one cutting area to another. Low Z clearances may speed up production slightly because the machine doesn't have to spend a lot of time raising and lowering the bit.

Even when hold-down clamps have been positioned out of the cutting area, you can still (literally) run into problems. This hold-down clamp's knob was in the way as an endmill moved to another area, and suffered as the endmill crashed into it and sliced out a chunk.

The damage would have been prevented by setting the Z Clearance high enough that the bit traveled above the knob.

Cam edge clamps

Edge clamps

Cam clamps can also be easily made on the CNC. They apply increasing pressure to the side of the workpiece as the cam is turned. These cams were designed to be held by short sections of 1/2" copper tubing that drop into pre-positioned holes in the spoilboard.

A jig or fixture system like this can speed setup when cutting multiples of identically-sized pieces.

Special edge clamps, like the one above, apply pressure both into and down on the edge of the material to hold it firmly in place. They work with T-track or can be bolted into appropriately-sized threaded inserts.

There are many more variations of clamping systems for the CNC. Large production shops often use vacuum holding for large sheets of material being cut into cabinets or other parts.

Vacuum holding requires more equipment and the creation of vacuum zones on the spoilboard, and may not be practical for small shops doing a variety of different projects. The methods we've discussed are more versatile and easier to use for most of us.

Quick repeat clamping with cams

DUST CONTROL

Be prepared, CNC is messy

The CNC router process is **subtractive**. That means you start with a block of material and remove everything you don't want. It's a little like carving a statue out of a block of marble, and boy can it be messy.

A dust boot helps collect the chips at the source

Even the simple process of cutting a few words into a sign with a V bit can throw a lot of sawdust and chips in all directions.

The mess can be mitigated somewhat with dust control or an enclosure, but you will still be cleaning up lots of waste material.

Some materials can be hazardous to your health, especially the MDF we're using for our spoilboards. Always wear a dust mask and eye protection when you're cutting it.

You've probably seen YouTube videos where someone is chasing the moving bit around with a shop vac nozzle to control the dust. They're doing that so you can see how the tool is machining the material, but it's a practice you should avoid. A moment's inattention or attempting to get closer to the spinning tool can lead to a collision between the bit and the vacuum nozzle.

A more common solution is adding a dust boot to your CNC. Dust boots do a good job of capturing the bulk of the sawdust and chips. The boot surrounds the bit and corrals the chips as they are cut so they can be sucked up by an attached vacuum or dust collector hose. The downside to dust boots is that you can't see what the bit is doing while it is cutting.

Simple dust shields or a full enclosure surrounding the CNC are an excellent way of controlling all the dust and chips while giving clear visibility of what the tool is doing. Dust ports for vacuum or dust collector hoses can be designed into an enclosure, or the waste can be easily vacuumed out of the enclosure when the job is completed.

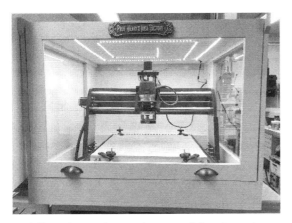

A full enclosure keeps the rest of the shop clean

BEWARE OF STATIC ELECTRICITY

Static discharges can be a killer of electrical devices like the controllers on our CNCs, and dust collection systems are the biggest producer of static in any workshop.

The CNC's electronics can be fried by merely vacuuming their components while they are on.

Static is produced by the air rushing through vacuum hoses and dust collector pipes. Plastic piping and hoses are the worst culprits, but metal ducting has problems also. All hoses and ducting should be grounded.

The simplest grounding method is a bare copper wire running through the ductwork and connected to an earth ground at one end. When metal ducting is grounded, it drains the static from the chips flowing through it to the dust control system.

Anti-static vacuum hose is available and can be used where the hose attaches to the CNC.

As a separate issue, the metal machine parts and any electrical boxes or cabinets should also be attached to a common earth ground also. You should consult the vendor of your machine for their recommendations.

ORGANIZE YOUR WORKSPACE

A lot is going on with your CNC. You've got hold down components, tool bits, bit changing tools, electronic wiring, router and spindle cables, stepper motor wiring, and more.

Keeping things organized will help you keep your area cleaner and simplify working with your CNC. Router bits, for example, multiply like rabbits as you do more projects, and you need a way to identify them quickly and store them safely. Throwing a handful of carbide edged bits into a box where they bang against one another is a sure way of ruining them. A few minutes getting organized will save hours of production time.

CHAPTER 6

Putting the CNC to work

Are we finally ready to make something?

Yes, we are. It's taken a while to get here, but now we can put all we've talked about into practice and get our CNC into production.

We discussed the basics of CNC machining, used our CAD software to design a sign project, and reviewed some basics about cutting tool selection. Then we created toolpaths with CAM software and exported the G-code for our machine to individual files, set up a spoilboard, talked about holding the material in place, how to deal with all the dust and chips we'll produce, plus talked briefly about the potential for damage from static electricity.

Recapping our address sign project, we will be cutting 3/4" thick material that measures 16" wide by 11.25" tall. We set the origin point of our design at the center and will cut the project with five toolpaths using an endmill, a V-bit, and a ballnose bit.

We'll need to mark the zero point for the workpiece and hold it down on the spoilboard, set the X, Y zero on the CNC, reset the Z-height after every tool change, and run the appropriate G-code file for each operation to complete our sign.

Let's head to the shop.

Marking the zero point

Since we set the origin point at the center of our material when we designed the sign, we mark the center of our sign blank by drawing diagonal lines from the corners so we can zero the X and Y axes at that point.

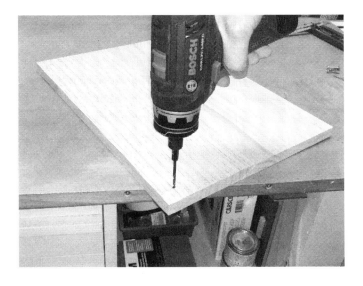

Drilling for hold down

We're going to use screws to hold our blank to the spoilboard. Pre-drilled pilot holes will keep the wood from splitting, and we can be sure they will be out of the way of any toolpaths.

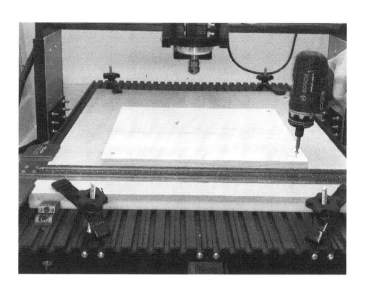

Squaring and securing the workpiece

A T-square is a quick and easy way to align our workpiece to the spoilboard. Then we can just screw the piece in place using our pre-drilled holes.

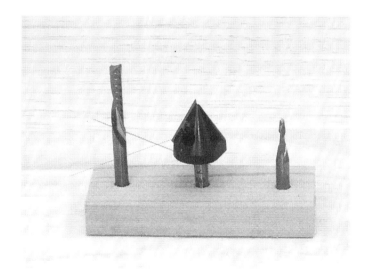

The tools

We only need three tools for this project. A 1/4" downcutting spiral endmill, a 60° V-bit, and a 1/8" ballnose.

Establishing X, Y zero

The X, Y zero needs to be set so the CNC knows where to start and end each operation. With a pointed v-bit in place, we manually jog the bit along the X and Y axes until it is over our center mark. Then we use our control software to set the X and Y axes at 0.

The router or spindle MUST BE OFF for all zeroing operations.

Z-zero by feel

With the X, Y zero set, it's time to set the Z zero for our first tool. We'll establish the zero as the top of the material because that's how we set it up in our design.

A simple method for setting the Z height is to slowly lower the bit onto a scrap of paper while sliding the paper back and forth. Set your Z at zero when the paper just drags against the bit.

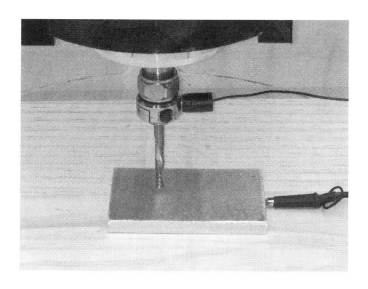

Z-zero by touch plate

A touch plate gives consistent results for setting the Z zero. A probe is attached to the bit or collet, and the controller software slowly lowers the bit until it touches the plate and makes electrical contact. The Z height is automatically established when you accept the detected setting.

Remember: You MUST RESET the Z height AFTER EACH TOOL CHANGE.

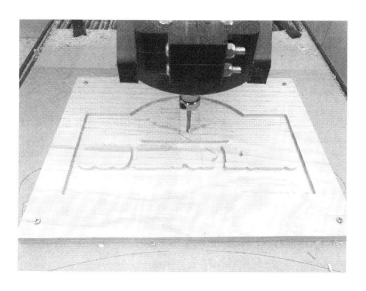

Clearing most of the pocket

Here's how the sign looks after running our first toolpath to clean out the majority of the background.

The 1/4" downcut spiral left clean edges on the top surface and a flat bottom for the next operations.

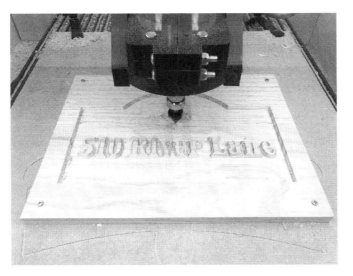

V-carving the address

After changing the tool to a 60°
V-bit and resetting the Z zero, we
ran the second part of the address
toolpath. Now our address text
has shape and dimension, and
the inside of our border has a nice
chamfer.

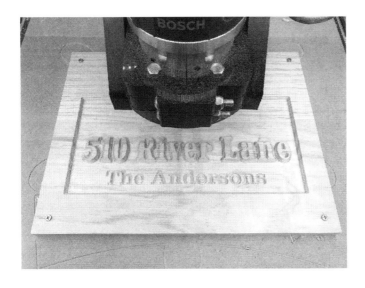

V-carving the name

The name was quickly carved into
the background without the need
for changing tools or resetting the
Z zero since it uses the same tool
as the address carving. The CNC
knows that our toolpath starts
machining 1/4" below the top
surface of the sign.

Carving the texture

After changing the tool to a 1/8″ ballnose and resetting the Z zero for the new tool, we ran the texture toolpath to create a worn woodgrain look.

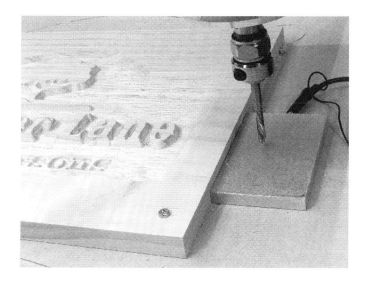

Setting Z for the cutout

We'll be cutting all the way through the material and slightly into the spoilboard to cut the outline.

By setting the Z-zero off of the spoilboard, we can compensate for the fact that the actual thickness of 3/4″ material can vary by several thousandths of an inch.

We'll use the controller to change this spoilboard zero reading to -.75″ instead of 0.0″, so our 3/4″ depth of cut will stop right at the surface of the spoilboard regardless of the board's actual thickness.

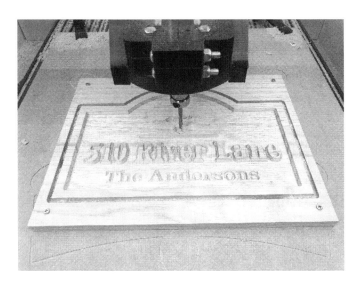

Cutout completed

The downcut spiral bit cut out our sign's shape leaving small tabs of material to prevent the sign breaking free from the screwed-down waste.

Removing the tabs

With the sign unscrewed and removed from the spoilboard, it's a quick operation to cut through the tabs and separate it from the waste material.

Sandpaper, a chisel, or a pattern bit in a hand-held router will quickly clean up any bits of leftover tabs sticking out from the sides.

We're done! We did it.

Remember how we started with only an idea and a bitmapped graphic of a tree? We converted the tree to vectors and resized it to fit in a sign panel vector provided by our CAD software. Then we added some text and moved on to the CAM software to create toolpaths that we cut with just three tools: a 1/4" endmill, a 60° V-bit, and 1/8" ballnose.

By securing the blank wood to our spoilboard and using tabs for the cutout profile, we kept the finished sign from flying loose when we completed the cut. Finally, we just trimmed off the tabs, and now it's time for a little sanding and finishing. Our sign can be left natural, varnished, stained, painted, or a combination of the options.

CHAPTER 7

Congratulations!

You have left the Newbie ranks and advanced to CNC Novice.

You now understand the basics of how CNC works, you know how a project is designed, and how to convert that design to coded instructions your CNC can follow. You're familiar with the various tool types and the kind of cuts they make, and seen how to apply them to a simple project.

You know how to determine the feed and speed settings for individual cutting tools, to ensure the best combination of quality of cut vs. production time.

You understand the importance of securing your work to a sacrificial table that can be easily constructed and maintained. You know how to hold the work in place, and the importance of dust collection to keep your work area clean.

You've seen how quickly you can produce an excellent looking product with only a few cutting tools, and you've learned some of the key vocabulary words that make up the lingo of CNC.

Do you know everything? Nope, but neither does anyone else. We should always be learning new techniques and working toward improving our CNC skills.

There's still a lot learn, like making double-side projects, 3-D carving, creating lithophanes, using tiling methods to cut projects larger than your machine's normal cutting area, and creating special jigs or fixtures to speed up production of multiples of the same part.

You've learned the basics, and your skills will improve with every project. The ability to create new and exciting projects is only limited by your imagination.

As a CNC Novice, you can approach the world of CNC with confidence, putting away all the trepidation and fear you had as a Newbie. Now, go out there and make something!

Appendix

Here's a Glossary of words YOU SHOULD KNOW

Aspire
CAD/CAM software from Vectric, Ltd. used to design and create G-code for CNC projects. Aspire can create 3-D models for CNC operations.

Ballnose bit
A bit with a rounded cutting end. Most commonly used for 3-D carving and texturing.

Bitmap
A digital image file format composed of a matrix of squares or pixels. Bitmaps must be changed to vectors for CNC work.

CAD
Computer Aided Design. You use CAD software to design your project.

CAM
Computer Aided Manufacturing. You use CAM software to convert your design to toolpaths for the CNC to follow.

Carbide
A hard material used extensively for cutting edge tools because it stays sharp longer than high-speed steel.

Carriage
The carriage is part of the gantry and holds the router of spindle. It generally moves side-to-side along the X axis.

Chip load
The thickness, or bite, of material removed by one cutting edge of the cutter as it rotates along the toolpath.

CNC
Computer Numerical Control. Meaning the tool is controlled by a computer following coded commands.

Collet
The collet is a segmented chuck that holds your tool in the router or spindle.

Compression bit   A bit with combined up cutting and down cutting spiral flutes. The up cutting flutes on the tip give clean cuts to the bottom of the material and the down cutting flutes give clean cuts on the surface.

Controller   The brain of the CNC system that links the mechanical components to the computer system.

Downcut spiral bit   The flutes push the chips down into to the groove made by the cutter. Leaves clean edges at the surface.

Feed Rate   The lateral speed a tool moves through the material during a cutting operation.

Finishing Toolpath   A toolpath generally using a smaller tool for finer detailed machining of 3-D objects.

Flute   The cutting edge of the router bit. The bit may have single or multiple flutes.

G-code   Geometric Code. The instructions that guide the CNC's operations.

Gantry   The rigid, movable bar holding the router or spindle carriage. It generally moves back and forth along the Y axis.

Jog, Jogging   Using control software to manually move the machine along any axis.

Leadscrew   Some machines use long threaded rods to control the movement along each axis. They translate rotary motion into linear motion.

Limit Switch   Some machines have a switch which detects when a machine reaches the end of travel along an axis.

LinuxCNC   An open-source CNC controller.

Mach 3 / Mach 4	CNC controller software by Artsoft a division of New Fangled Solutions.
Pendant	A hand-held control device for a CNC machine to move the machines axes and start and stop toolpaths.
Post Processor	A driver that works with CAM software to create the correct G-code for a specific CNC machine.
Rack and pinion	Some machines use gears to drive the axes rather than leadscrews.
Roughing Toolpath	A roughing toolpath, usually with a large diameter tool, removes a lot of waste material in preparation for a finishing toolpath.
RPM	Revolutions Per Minute. The rotation speed of a tool.
Shank	The part of a cutting tool that is held by the collet.
Spindle	Some machines use a spindle in place of a router. Spindles run quieter than routers and can be water cooled.
Spiral bit	A bit where the flutes wrap around the diameter of the tool for smoother cutting.
Spoilboard	A sacrificial top that protects your machine table from damage, especially when machining through the thickness of your stock.
TAP	A file format for the G-code which runs the toolpath you set up in your design software.
Tapered Ballnose	A ballnose bit that tapers from a narrow cutting point to the diameter of the shaft. Most commonly found on bits with small cutting diameters of 1/16" or less.
Tool	The tool or router bit used for machining a toolpath.

Toolpath   The path the tool will follow to cut or carve, guided by the code generated by your CAM software.

Touchplate   An accessory for most machines that allows quick and consistent setting of the Z zero for a tool operation by detecting when the tool touches the plate.

Turbo-CNC   CNC control software from DAK Engineering

Upcut spiral bit   The flutes pull the chips up to the surface of the material. May roughen the cut edges at the surface.

V Carve   CAD/CAM software from Vectric, Ltd. used to design and create G-code for CNC projects. Available in Desktop and Pro versions.

Vector   A mathematically defined line or shape created by design programs and can be infinitely scaled without loss of quality. CAD software creates vectors the CAM software uses to define toolpaths.

X-Axis   The X Axis is the right to left movement of your machine.

Y-Axis   The Y Axis is the front to back movement of your machine.

Z-Axis   The Z-Axis is the up and down movement of your router or spindle.

Zero   The Zero postion is the spot on your work where all movement, X, Y, and Z originate. It is defined when you set up your job in your design software. Sometimes referred to as the Home postion.

V-Bit Cutting Depths / Widths

These V-bit cutting depths aren't exact due to rounding to three decimals, but they'll get you in the ballpark when you want to compare the cutting depths of bits for a known cutting width. Or, use the table get an approximation of how wide a cut a V-bit will make at a given depth.

Cutting Depths

Cutting Width	30° V-Bit	45° V-Bit	60° V-Bit	90° V-Bit
0.005	0.009	0.006	0.004	0.003
0.010	0.019	0.012	0.009	0.005
0.020	0.037	0.024	0.017	0.010
0.030	0.056	0.036	0.026	0.015
0.040	0.075	0.048	0.035	0.020
0.050	0.093	0.060	0.043	0.025
0.060	0.112	0.072	0.052	0.030
0.070	0.131	0.084	0.061	0.035
0.080	0.149	0.097	0.069	0.040
0.090	0.168	0.109	0.078	0.045
0.100	0.187	0.121	0.087	0.050
0.200	0.373	0.241	0.173	0.100
0.300	0.560	0.362	0.260	0.150
0.400	0.746	0.483	0.346	0.200
0.500	0.933	0.604	0.433	0.250
0.600	1.120	0.724	0.520	0.300
0.700	1.306	0.845	0.606	0.350
0.800	1.493	0.966	0.693	0.400
0.900	1.679	1.086	0.779	0.450
1.000	1.866	1.207	0.866	0.500

Speed and Feeds Test Results

CNC Model:

DATE	BIT	FEED RATE	RPM	MATERIAL

NOTES: ☐POOR ☐ GOOD ☐ EXCELLENT

DATE	BIT	FEED RATE	RPM	MATERIAL

NOTES: ☐POOR ☐ GOOD ☐ EXCELLENT

DATE	BIT	FEED RATE	RPM	MATERIAL

NOTES: ☐POOR ☐ GOOD ☐ EXCELLENT

DATE	BIT	FEED RATE	RPM	MATERIAL

NOTES: ☐POOR ☐ GOOD ☐ EXCELLENT

DATE	BIT	FEED RATE	RPM	MATERIAL

NOTES: ☐POOR ☐ GOOD ☐ EXCELLENT

DATE	BIT	FEED RATE	RPM	MATERIAL

NOTES: ☐POOR ☐ GOOD ☐ EXCELLENT

DATE	BIT	FEED RATE	RPM	MATERIAL

NOTES: ☐POOR ☐ GOOD ☐ EXCELLENT

Speed and Feeds Test Results

CNC Model:

DATE	BIT	FEED RATE	RPM	MATERIAL

NOTES: ☐POOR ☐ GOOD ☐ EXCELLENT

DATE	BIT	FEED RATE	RPM	MATERIAL

NOTES: ☐POOR ☐ GOOD ☐ EXCELLENT

DATE	BIT	FEED RATE	RPM	MATERIAL

NOTES: ☐POOR ☐ GOOD ☐ EXCELLENT

DATE	BIT	FEED RATE	RPM	MATERIAL

NOTES: ☐POOR ☐ GOOD ☐ EXCELLENT

DATE	BIT	FEED RATE	RPM	MATERIAL

NOTES: ☐POOR ☐ GOOD ☐ EXCELLENT

DATE	BIT	FEED RATE	RPM	MATERIAL

NOTES: ☐POOR ☐ GOOD ☐ EXCELLENT

DATE	BIT	FEED RATE	RPM	MATERIAL

NOTES: ☐POOR ☐ GOOD ☐ EXCELLENT

Speed and Feeds Test Results

CNC Model:

DATE	BIT	FEED RATE	RPM	MATERIAL

NOTES: ☐ POOR ☐ GOOD ☐ EXCELLENT

DATE	BIT	FEED RATE	RPM	MATERIAL

NOTES: ☐ POOR ☐ GOOD ☐ EXCELLENT

DATE	BIT	FEED RATE	RPM	MATERIAL

NOTES: ☐ POOR ☐ GOOD ☐ EXCELLENT

DATE	BIT	FEED RATE	RPM	MATERIAL

NOTES: ☐ POOR ☐ GOOD ☐ EXCELLENT

DATE	BIT	FEED RATE	RPM	MATERIAL

NOTES: ☐ POOR ☐ GOOD ☐ EXCELLENT

DATE	BIT	FEED RATE	RPM	MATERIAL

NOTES: ☐ POOR ☐ GOOD ☐ EXCELLENT

DATE	BIT	FEED RATE	RPM	MATERIAL

NOTES: ☐ POOR ☐ GOOD ☐ EXCELLENT

Speed and Feeds Test Results

CNC Model:

DATE	BIT	FEED RATE	RPM	MATERIAL

NOTES: ☐POOR ☐ GOOD ☐ EXCELLENT

DATE	BIT	FEED RATE	RPM	MATERIAL

NOTES: ☐POOR ☐ GOOD ☐ EXCELLENT

DATE	BIT	FEED RATE	RPM	MATERIAL

NOTES: ☐POOR ☐ GOOD ☐ EXCELLENT

DATE	BIT	FEED RATE	RPM	MATERIAL

NOTES: ☐POOR ☐ GOOD ☐ EXCELLENT

DATE	BIT	FEED RATE	RPM	MATERIAL

NOTES: ☐POOR ☐ GOOD ☐ EXCELLENT

DATE	BIT	FEED RATE	RPM	MATERIAL

NOTES: ☐POOR ☐ GOOD ☐ EXCELLENT

DATE	BIT	FEED RATE	RPM	MATERIAL

NOTES: ☐POOR ☐ GOOD ☐ EXCELLENT

Speed and Feeds Test Results

CNC Model:

DATE	BIT	FEED RATE	RPM	MATERIAL

NOTES: ☐POOR ☐ GOOD ☐ EXCELLENT

DATE	BIT	FEED RATE	RPM	MATERIAL

NOTES: ☐POOR ☐ GOOD ☐ EXCELLENT

DATE	BIT	FEED RATE	RPM	MATERIAL

NOTES: ☐POOR ☐ GOOD ☐ EXCELLENT

DATE	BIT	FEED RATE	RPM	MATERIAL

NOTES: ☐POOR ☐ GOOD ☐ EXCELLENT

DATE	BIT	FEED RATE	RPM	MATERIAL

NOTES: ☐POOR ☐ GOOD ☐ EXCELLENT

DATE	BIT	FEED RATE	RPM	MATERIAL

NOTES: ☐POOR ☐ GOOD ☐ EXCELLENT

DATE	BIT	FEED RATE	RPM	MATERIAL

NOTES: ☐POOR ☐ GOOD ☐ EXCELLENT

Speed and Feeds Test Results

CNC Model:

DATE	BIT	FEED RATE	RPM	MATERIAL

NOTES: ☐POOR ☐ GOOD ☐ EXCELLENT

DATE	BIT	FEED RATE	RPM	MATERIAL

NOTES: ☐POOR ☐ GOOD ☐ EXCELLENT

DATE	BIT	FEED RATE	RPM	MATERIAL

NOTES: ☐POOR ☐ GOOD ☐ EXCELLENT

DATE	BIT	FEED RATE	RPM	MATERIAL

NOTES: ☐POOR ☐ GOOD ☐ EXCELLENT

DATE	BIT	FEED RATE	RPM	MATERIAL

NOTES: ☐POOR ☐ GOOD ☐ EXCELLENT

DATE	BIT	FEED RATE	RPM	MATERIAL

NOTES: ☐POOR ☐ GOOD ☐ EXCELLENT

DATE	BIT	FEED RATE	RPM	MATERIAL

NOTES: ☐POOR ☐ GOOD ☐ EXCELLENT

INDEX

Printed in Great Britain
by Amazon